Look, I Can Talk!

Student Notebook

(Available in English, Spanish, French, German)

A Step-By-Step Approach To Communication
Through TPR Stories

BY

BLAINE RAY

Edited by James J. Asher

Illustrated by Greg Rowe

Look, I Can Talk!
Student Notebook in English

BY
BLAINE RAY

Edited by James J. Asher

Illustrated by Greg Rowe

Published by
Sky Oaks Productions, Inc.

P.O. Box 1102
Los Gatos, CA 95031-1102
TEL (408) 395-7600
FAX (408) 395-8440

© Copyright, 1990, 1991

ISBN 1-56018-456-6

Free TPR Catalog upon request!

TABLE OF CONTENTS

CHAPTER ONE

THE CAT STORY

VOCABULARY

THE CAT STORY

VOCABULARY

1 bad boy   2 cat   3 girl   4 grabs   5 little   6 big

7 runs away   8 throws   9 cries   10 gives   11 the girl laughs

12 sad girl   13 happy boy 14 floor

15 good   16 runs   17 sees

THE CAT STORY

THE CAT STORY

There is a girl. Her name is Tami. She has a big cat.

There is a boy. His name is Craig. He is a bad boy. He runs to the girl and grabs the cat and throws the cat on the floor. The cat runs away. The girl is very sad. She cries and cries, but Craig laughs.

There is another girl. Her name is Monica. Monica sees that Tami is crying. Tami is crying because she doesn't have a cat. Monica runs to Tami and gives her the cat. Tami is very happy now.

EXERCISE 1

WRITE TRUE OR FALSE TO THE LEFT OF THE NUMBER.

____ 1. The girl's name is Tami.
____ 2. The girl has a dog.
____ 3. The cat throws the dog.
____ 4. There is a boy and his name is Craig.
____ 5. Craig is a good boy.

____ 6. Craig runs away.
____ 7. Craig throws the cat.
____ 8. The other girl's name is Monica.
____ 9. Monica cries.
____ 10. Tami gives the cat to Monica

EXERCISE 2

FILL IN THE BLANKS WITH A WORD THAT MAKES THE SENTENCE TRUE.

1. The girl's name is _____.
2. _____ has a cat.
3. Tami has a _____ cat.
4. Craig is a bad _____.
5. Craig throws the cat on the _____.
6. The _____ runs away.

7. Tami _____ but Craig laughs.
8. _____ is the name of the other girl.
9. Monica runs to Tami and gives her a
    _____.
10. Tami is very _____ because
    she has another cat.

EXERCISE 3

PUT THESE SENTENCES IN THE CORRECT ORDER.

____ Tami has a cat.
____ The boy throws the cat on the floor.
____ Craig is a bad boy.
____ Craig grabs the cat.

____ Monica has a cat.
____ Monica gives the cat to Tami.
____ The cat runs away.
____ Tami is happy because she has
     another cat.

4

EXERCISE 4
ANSWER THE QUESTIONS WITH SHORT ANSWERS.
(IF THE ANSWER ISN'T IN THE STORY, MAKE IT UP.)

1. What is the name of the girl?

2. Why does she have a cat?

3. What is the name of the boy?

4. Why is the boy bad?

5. Who throws the cat on the floor?

6. Does the boy run away or does the cat run away?

7. Why is the girl sad?

8. Why does the cat run away?

9. What is the name of the other girl?

10. What does Monica give Tami?

EXERCISE 5

REWRITE THE STORY IN YOUR OWN WORDS.

_____

_____

_____

_____

_____

_____

_____

1

2

RETELL THIS VERSION.

VERSION A

3

4

5

6

EXERCISE 8

WRITE YOUR OWN STORY.

_____

_____

_____

_____

_____

_____

_____

EXERCISE 9

RETELL THE FOLLOWING STORIES.

1. The cat jumps on a boat and goes to China.

2. Two girls have a cat. The cat runs away. A boy grabs the cat and gives the cat to another girl.

3. Two boys take a cat. They throw the cat. The cat jumps on a little girl. The little girl is happy. She pets the cat.

4. The girl sees a cat and throws it.

5. The cat runs to the boy. The boy grabs the cat and runs away.

6. The boy sees two cats. He grabs one cat. The other cat runs away. The boy runs to a girl. He gives her the cat.

7. Monica is sad. She doesn't have a cat. A cat runs to Monica. Monica grabs the cat. She is happy.

8. Tami is on the floor. Two cats are on Tami. One is big and one is little. The little cat runs away.

9. Tami is a good girl. Monica is a bad girl. Monica grabs Tami's cat. Tami cries.

10. A little boy has a cat. He is happy. The cat runs away. He is sad.

CHAPTER TWO

THE COW AND THE MONKEY

VOCABULARY

THE COW AND THE MONKEY

VOCABULARY

1 bed

2 dry

3 house

4 poor

5 monkey sleeps

6 has

7 excited

8 rich

9 cow

10 snores

11 day

12 fat

13 loud

14 shoes

15 street

16 wakes up

THE COW AND THE MONKEY

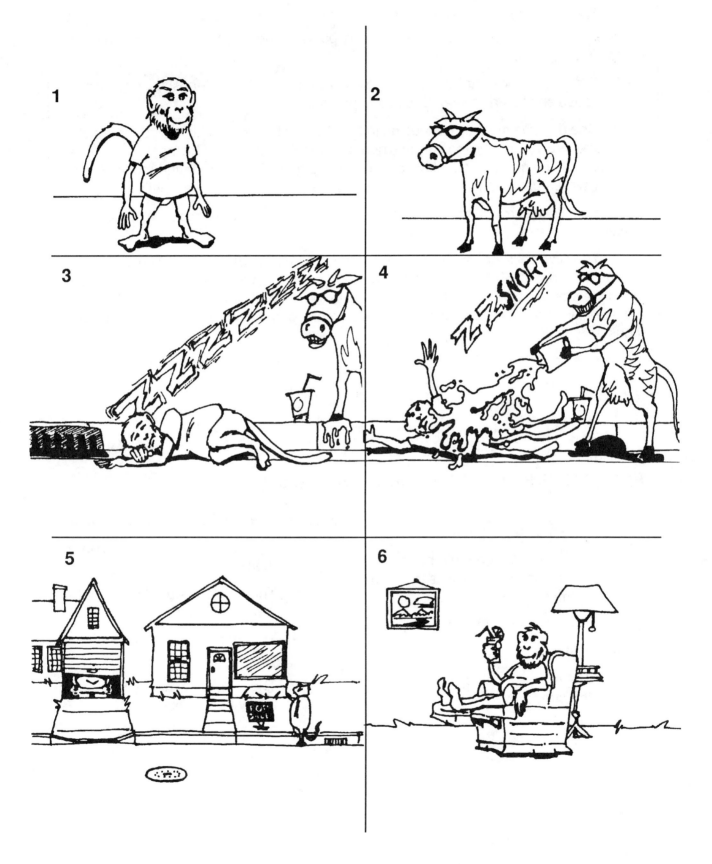

THE COW AND THE MONKEY

There is a monkey who is very different. He is tall, and he doesn't have any shoes. He doesn't have any shoes because he is very poor. He doesn't have a house either. He sleeps in the street.

There is a cow. She is a little fat. She has a house. She sleeps in a bed. She is rich because she has a house. She is a happy cow.

One day, the monkey is sleeping in the street. He is snoring. The cow is walking on the street. She sees the monkey and hears the monkey snoring. The monkey is snoring very loudly. The cow takes a glass of water and throws the water on the monkey. The monkey wakes up. The monkey is very mad because he is wet. The cow is dry.

He tells the cow, "I am a poor monkey. I sleep in the street because I don't have a house."

The cow looks for a house for the monkey. The cow finds a house. The cow is very excited and happy. She goes to the monkey and says, "I have a house for you." The cow takes the monkey by the hand and takes him to the house. The cow gives the house to the monkey. The monkey is happy. He doesn't sleep in the street now. He is a normal monkey.

EXERCISE 1

WRITE TRUE OR FALSE TO THE LEFT OF THE NUMBER.

_____ 1. The monkey is poor.

_____ 2. The monkey doesn't have any shoes because he has a lot of money.

_____ 3. The monkey has a house.

_____ 4. The cow sleeps in a bed.

_____ 5. The monkey is sleeping in a bed in the street.

_____ 6. The monkey snores really loudly.

_____ 7. The cow pours water on the monkey.

_____ 8. The monkey is mad because he is wet.

_____ 9. The monkey finds a house for the cow.

_____ 10. The monkey is happy because he finally has a house.

12

EXERCISE 2

FILL IN THE BLANKS WITH A WORD THAT MAKES THE SENTENCE TRUE.

1. The monkey doesn't have any
   _____.

2. The monkey has no money and sleeps
   in the _____.

3. The monkey doesn't have a _____.

4. The cow has a _____.

5. The monkey _____ really loudly.

6. The cow throws _____ on the
   monkey.

7. The monkey is mad at the cow because
   he is _____.

8. The cow looks for a _____ for
   the monkey.

9. The cow takes the _____ to his
   new house.

10. The cow _____ the house to
    the monkey.

EXERCISE 3

ANSWER THE QUESTIONS WITH SHORT ANSWERS.
(IF THE ANSWER ISN'T IN THE STORY, MAKE IT UP.)

1. Why doesn't the monkey have a house?

2. Where does the monkey sleep?

3. Why does the monkey sleep in the street?

4. Why is the cow rich?

5. Why does the cow throw water on the
   monkey?

6. Why does the monkey get mad?

7. Why does the monkey wake up?

8. Why does the cow sleep in the bed?

9. Why is the cow excited and happy?

10. Why does the monkey have a house?

EXERCISE 4

PUT THESE SENTENCES IN THE CORRECT ORDER.

_____ The cow throws water on the
      monkey.

_____ There is a monkey.

_____ The monkey snores loudly.

_____ The monkey is happy because he
      has a house.

_____ There is a cow.

_____ The cow looks for a house for the
      monkey.

13

EXERCISE 5

REWRITE THE STORY IN YOUR OWN WORDS.

_____

_____

_____

_____

_____

_____

EXERCISE 6

RETELL THIS VERSION.

VERSION A

EXERCISE 8

WRITE YOUR OWN STORY.

_____

_____

_____

_____

_____

_____

_____

_____

EXERCISE 9

RETELL THE FOLLOWING STORIES.

1. The monkey is rich and the cow is poor.

2. A cat sleeps in the street. A boy throws water on the cat. The cat wakes up and runs away. The boy goes to his house.

3. The monkey has a house. He is sleeping in a bed. The cow goes to the monkey's house. The cow screams. The monkey wakes up. The monkey is mad.

4. The cow has four shoes. She sees the monkey in the street. The monkey has no shoes. She gives the monkey two shoes. The monkey has two shoes and the cow has two shoes.

5. The cow sees the monkey in the street. The monkey wakes up and goes to the cow's house. The monkey sleeps in the cow's house and doesn't sleep in the street.

6. The cow throws water on the monkey. The monkey throws water on the cow. They are wet. They look for a house for the monkey. They see a house. The monkey sleeps in the house.

7. Two monkeys are sleeping in the street. They tell the cow they have a house. The cow says, "Good bye." The monkeys are sad because they really don't have a house.

8. The cow is a bad cow and laughs at the monkey. The monkey cries and runs away. He is sad. He goes to California. He sleeps on the street in California.

9. The boy doesn't have a bed. He sleeps on the floor. He looks for a bed. He finds a bed. He sleeps in the bed.

10. The cow gives the monkey a lot of money and the monkey buys his own house.

16

THE LOST BOOK

VOCABULARY

CHAPTER THREE

THE LOST BOOK

VOCABULARY

1 TABLE

2 LIGHT

3 PICKS UP

4 OPEN

5 STANDS UP

6 MOM

7 MAGAZINE

8 CLOSED, CORNER

9 BOOK

10 SITS DOWN

11 WINDOW

12 HAND

13 SCHOOL

THE LOST BOOK

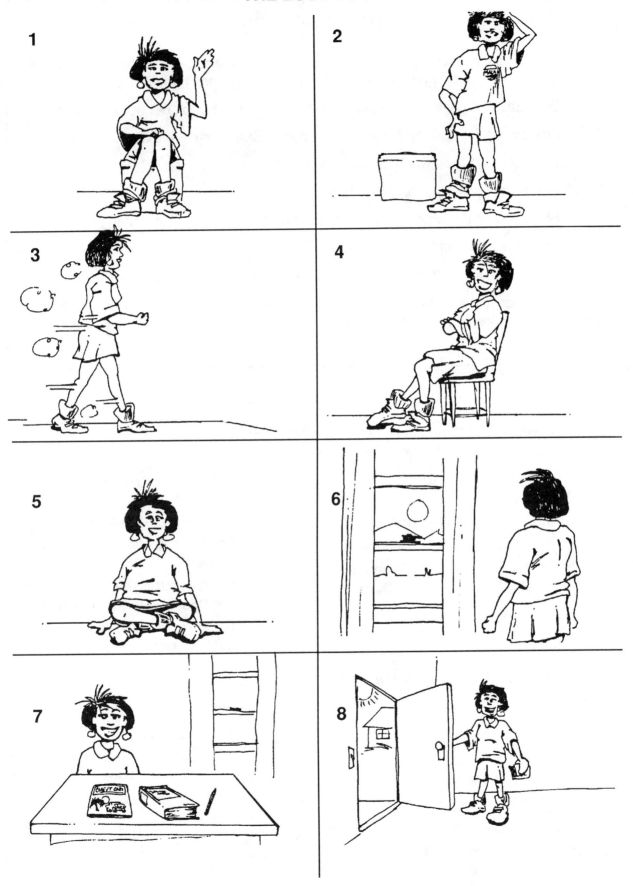

THE LOST BOOK

There is a girl. Her name is Susan. She stands up and says, "Where is my book?" She walks to the corner and looks for the book, but she doesn't find it.

She runs to a chair and sits down. She looks for the book but doesn't find it.

She sits on the floor and looks for the book. She doesn't find it.

She yells, "Mother, where is my book?"

Her mother screams, "Look for it by the window!"

She walks to the window and looks for it by the window. She doesn't find it.

She says, "Mother, it is not here."

Her mother says, "Look for it on the table between the magazine and the pencil."

She goes to the table and finds it between the magazine and the pencil. She walks to the door and yells, "Bye, Mother." She goes to the door and opens it. She leaves but she doesn't close the door. She goes to school.

EXERCISE 1

WRITE TRUE OR FALSE TO THE LEFT OF THE NUMBER.

_____ 1. The name of the girl is Susan.

_____ 2. Susan's book is on her head.

_____ 3. Susan jumps to the chair.

_____ 4. The girl laughs at her mother.

_____ 5. Susan asks her mom, "Where is my book?"

_____ 6. Her mother says that the book is on the table.

_____ 7. Susan throws the book on the floor.

_____ 8. The book is between a light and a magazine.

_____ 9. Susan puts the book on her shoulder and leaves the house.

_____ 10. Susan opens the door and walks out the door.

EXERCISE 2

WRITE A WORD THAT MAKES THE SENTENCE TRUE.

1. The name of the girl is _____.

2. Susan _____ to the wall.

3. Susan runs to the _____.

4. The girl sits on the _____.

5. "Mother, where is my _____?"

6. Her mother says it is between the _____ and the _____.

7. The book is on the _____.

8. Susan runs to the table and _____ her book.

9. The girl picks up the book and puts it in her _____.

10. She opens the door, walks out, and goes to _____.

EXERCISE 3

ANSWER THE QUESTIONS WITH SHORT ANSWERS.
(IF THE ANSWER ISN'T IN THE STORY, MAKE IT UP.)

1. What is the name of the girl?

2. What is the girl looking for?

3. Why is she looking for the book?

4. Who screams?

5. What does she scream?

6. Why does she sit on the floor?

7. Who tells Susan that the book is on the table?

8. Where does she find the book?

9. Why does she look for the book on the table?

10. Why does Susan go to school?

EXERCISE 4

PUT THESE SENTENCES IN THE CORRECT ORDER.

_____ The book is on the table next to the magazine.
_____ Susan leaves and goes to school.
_____ She doesn't see the book on the floor.
_____ The name of the girl is Susan.

_____ She doesn't have her book.
_____ She walks to the window.
_____ Susan goes to the corner.
_____ She sits on the chair.

EXERCISE 5

REWRITE THE STORY IN YOUR OWN WORDS.

_____

_____

_____

_____

_____

_____

_____

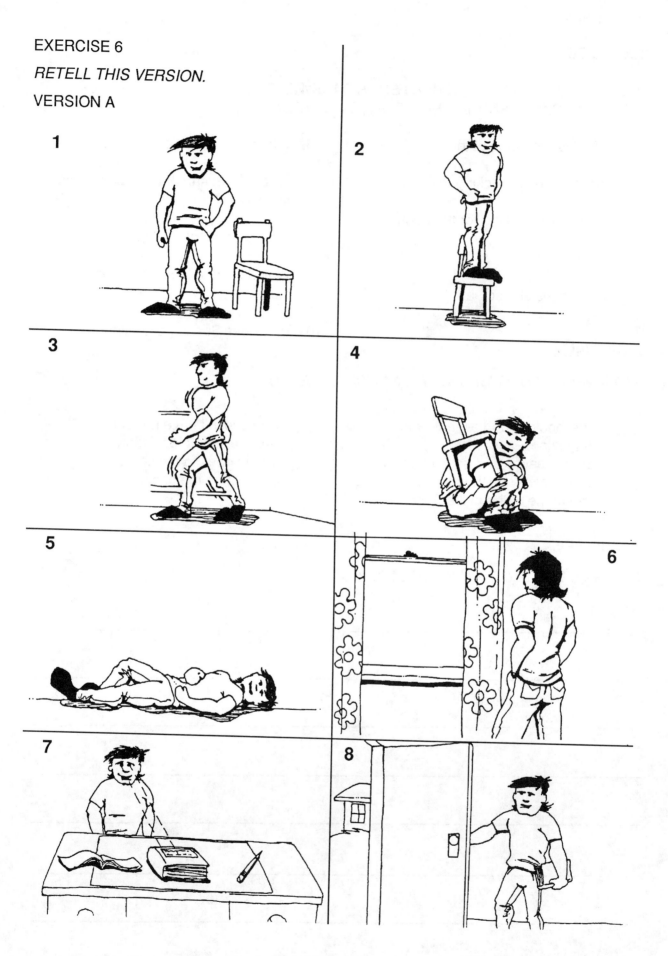

EXERCISE 7

VERSION B

1

2

3

4

5

6

7

8

23

EXERCISE 8

WRITE YOUR OWN STORY.

_____

_____

_____

_____

_____

_____

_____

EXERCISE 9

RETELL THE FOLLOWING STORIES.

1. The girl is a boy and his name is Ed. He finds his book on the floor.

2. Susan finds the book on the floor. She puts the book on the table and goes to school. She doesn't have the book at school. She goes home and gets the book. She goes to school with the book.

3. Susan walks to her mother and asks her mother where the book is. Her mother has the book and gives it to her. She puts the book on the floor and sits on it.

4. Susan is at school. She doesn't have her book. She looks for her book. She finds the book on her chair. She picks up the book and opens it. She is happy because she has her book.

5. The girl is walking on the street. She sees a book. She picks it up. She goes to school.

6. Her mother looks for the book by the window and on the floor. She finds it on the floor and puts it on the table. Susan goes to the table and picks up the book.

7. There are three books: one by the window, one on the floor, and one under the table. Susan only finds two of them. She doesn't find the one under the table. She goes to a girl's house with the two books in her hand.

8. Her mother puts the book by the table. She tells Susan to look for the book on the table. Susan finds the book on top of the table and yells, "Mother, the book is on top of the table." Susan picks up the book and leaves the house.

9. The girl looks for the book, but doesn't find it. She goes to school without it. A cat is sleeping at school. She sees the cat. The cat is sleeping on her book. She grabs the book. The cat wakes up and runs away.

10. Susan finds a book on the chair, but it is a different book. She finds another book on the floor, but it isn't her book. She finds a book on the table. It is her book. She is happy because she has the right book.

THE CLOTHING STORE

VOCABULARY

1	2	3

4	5	6	7

8	9	10	11

12	13	14	15

16	17	18

THE CLOTHING STORE

VOCABULARY

1 BEAUTIFUL   2 BUY   3 CLOTHING

4 ENTER   5 SECTION   6 SKIRT   7 SOCKS

8 SUIT   9 SHIRT   10 BLOUSE   11 DRESS

12 PANTS   13 BILL   14 CLERK   15 TRIES ON

16 HELPS   17 STORE   18 WANTS

THE CLOTHING STORE

Travis and Kim are walking along a street. They look down and find a pile of money. They say, "Great, let's go to a clothing store." They go into a clothing store.

Travis goes to the section of the store that has boy's clothing. He sees some pants that he likes. He tries them on. He says, "I want them." He tries on a shirt and some socks. He tries on a suit. He then tells the clerk, "I want the suit, the shirt, and the socks." Next, he goes to the shoe department. He tries on some shoes and says, "I want these shoes."

Kim goes to the girl's clothing department. A clerk there helps her. She tries on a beautiful dress. She says, "I want it." She tries on a blouse, a skirt, and some pants. She tells the clerk that she wants the blouse, the skirt, and the pants.

The clerk gives them the bill for the clothes. The clothes cost $295. They give him the pile of money. He counts the money. There is only $100. Kim says, "We will be right back. We will go find $200 more."

EXERCISE 1

WRITE TRUE OR FALSE TO THE LEFT OF THE NUMBER.

_____ 1. Travis is a girl and Kim is a boy.

_____ 2. They find ten dollars on the road.

_____ 3. They go to a restaurant and buy food.

_____ 4. They go to a clothing store to buy clothing.

_____ 5. Travis wants to buy shoes.

_____ 6. Kim wants to buy a dress.

_____ 7. Kim goes to the boy's clothing department.

_____ 8. Travis tries on a suit, but he doesn't want to buy it.

_____ 9. The total cost of the clothing is $295.

_____ 10. They don't have enough money to buy the clothes.

EXERCISE 2

FILL IN THE BLANKS WITH A WORD THAT MAKES THE SENTENCE TRUE.

1. Travis and Kim are walking along a _____.

2. They find a pile of _____ on the street.

3. They go to a _____ store.

4. Travis tries on some _____ .

5. Travis tells the _____ that he wants the shoes.

6. Kim tries on a _____ dress.

7. She also tries on some _____ .

8. The total _____ is $295.

9. They only _____ $100.

10. They will come back when they find more _____ .

EXERCISE 3

ANSWER THE QUESTIONS WITH SHORT ANSWERS.
(IF THE ANSWER ISN'T IN THE STORY, MAKE IT UP.)

1. Where are Travis and Kim walking?

2. How do they find the $100?

3. Why do they go to the clothing store?

4. Why do they try on the clothing?

5. Who tries on a suit?

6. Who goes to the girl's clothing department?

7. Who tries on the dress?

8. Why does Kim try on the shoes?

9. Why don't they buy the clothes?

10. Where are they going to get the rest of the money?

EXERCISE 4

PUT THESE SENTENCES IN THE CORRECT ORDER.

____ Kim wants to buy a dress, a blouse, and some pants.

____ Travis and Kim find $100.

____ Kim and Travis are walking along a street.

____ The bill is $295.

____ Travis wants to buy two suits, some shoes and socks.

____ They go to a clothing store.

____ Travis and Kim look for more money.

____ They only have $100.

EXERCISE 5

REWRITE THE STORY IN YOUR OWN WORDS.

_____

_____

_____

_____

_____

_____

EXERCISE 6

RETELL THIS VERSION.

VERSION A

1

2

3

4

5

6

1

2

3

4

5

6

EXERCISE 8

WRITE YOUR OWN STORY.

_____

_____

_____

_____

_____

_____

_____

EXERCISE 9

RETELL THE FOLLOWING STORIES.

1. Travis and Kim find $1000 and buy clothing. They now have $500 and go to Mexico. They buy more clothing in Mexico.

2. They leave and find the other $200. They return and buy the clothing.

3. They go to the clothing store and try on the clothing but they don't like it. They don't buy the clothing. They go to another store and buy a computer.

4. They find $100 and they go out and eat. They spend $50 on food. They give away the rest of the money to a man they see on the street. He goes to a restaurant and buys a good meal.

5. Kim gives the money to Travis and he buys a lot of clothes. Kim doesn't buy anything. Kim is mad because there is no more money.

6. They go to Pizza Hut and buy ten pizzas. They eat five of the pizzas and give five pizzas to other people in the restaurant.

7. Travis and Kim go to Japan. They enter a clothing store. The clothing costs a lot. They don't buy clothing. They go to a park. It is beautiful.

8. Travis and Kim buy a car. They go to New York. The car breaks down in New York. They sell the car. They take a train home.

9. Travis and Kim find a lot of money. They buy a clothing store. They sell lots of clothing. They buy more clothing stores. They become very rich.

10. When they are walking to the clothing store, a robber steals the money. They call the police. The police don't find the robbers. Travis and Kim look for the robbers. They see the robbers in the park. Travis and Kim scream. The police come and pick up the robbers.

THE LOTTERY TICKET

VOCABULARY

CHAPTER FIVE
THE LOTTERY TICKET
VOCABULARY

1 BED

2 JEWELRY

3 NIGHT

4 READS

5 THINKS

6 PAYS

7 BILLS

8 PARENTS

9 TICKET

10 CAR

11 NUMBERS

12 PUTS

13. WATCHES TV

THE LOTTERY TICKET

THE LOTTERY TICKET

A boy named Nick finds a lottery ticket. Nick is twelve years old. He looks at the numbers on the ticket and reads them. The numbers are 12-15-18-24-33-4 1. He watches TV that night. He sees the lottery numbers. They are 12-15-18-24-33-4 1. He wins a million dollars. There is a problem. He thinks his parents are going to take his money. He gets the money and puts it under his bed. The next day he spends a lot of the money. He buys jewelry, houses, and cars. He gives everything to his friends.

Finally, he only has a hundred dollars left. He takes the money to his mom and says, "Mom, look! I won a hundred dollars in the lottery." The mom is really happy and says, "That is your money and you can spend it any way you want."

EXERCISE 1

WRITE TRUE OR FALSE TO THE LEFT OF THE NUMBER.

_____ 1. The name of the boy is Fred.

_____ 2. The boy buys a lottery ticket.

_____ 3. The boy watches TV that night.

_____ 4. He wins $100.

_____ 5. He thinks his parents are going to give him more money.

_____ 6. He puts the money under the bed.

_____ 7. He buys houses, cars and jewelry.

_____ 8. He gives everything to his parents.

_____ 9. He tells his mom that he won a million dollars.

_____ 10. His mom says he can spend the money any way he wants.

EXERCISE 2

FILL IN THE BLANKS WITH A WORD THAT MAKES IT TRUE

1. Nick finds a lottery _____.

2. He looks at the numbers and _____ them.

3. He knows he wins when he watches _____ at night.

4. He _____ a million dollars.

5. He thinks his mom and dad are going to _____ the money.

6. Nick puts the money under his _____

7. He buys cars, jewelry and _____ .

8. He _____ his friends everything.

9. When he goes to his mom he only has one _____ dollars.

10. His mom lets him spend the _____ any way he wants.

EXERCISE 3

ANSWER THE QUESTIONS WITH SHORT ANSWERS.
(IF THE ANSWER ISN'T IN THE STORY, MAKE IT UP.)

1. Who finds a lottery ticket?

2. Why doesn't he buy a lottery ticket?

3. Why does Nick watch TV that night?

4. Why does he put the money under his bed?

5. Why does he spend the money?

6. What does he do with the money?

7. Why does he buy cars, houses, and jewelry?

8. Why did he tell his mom about the last $100?

9. Why doesn't his mom take the money?

10. What is Nick going to do the next time he wins a million dollars in the lottery?

EXERCISE 4

PUT THESE SENTENCES IN THE CORRECT ORDER.

_____Nick talks to his mom.

_____He watches TV.

_____The numbers are 12-15-18-24-33-4 1.

_____The boy wins $1,000,000.

_____Nick only has $100 left.

_____He finds a lottery ticket.

_____He gives everything away.

_____He buys cars, jewelry, and houses.

EXERCISE 5

REWRITE THE STORY IN YOUR OWN WORDS.

_____

_____

_____

_____

_____

_____

EXERCISE 6

RETELL THIS VERSION.

VERSION A

1

2

3

4

5

6

7

8

EXERCISE 8

WRITE YOUR OWN STORY.

_____

_____

_____

_____

_____

_____

_____

EXERCISE 9

RETELL THE FOLLOWING STORIES.

1. Nick tells his mom about the money and she takes the money. She leaves the country and goes to Mexico. She never goes back home.

2. Nick wins $1,000 in the lottery. He buys a car. He goes to his friend's house. They go to a store.

3. He gives the money to his parents and they buy him a new house and a new car. They put a lot of money in the bank. They go to Spain and France. They live there for two years.

4. He gets the money, but he goes to Las Vegas and loses all of the money. He walks home.

5. He goes to Europe, Asia and Africa with the money and takes his parents with him. They buy a hotel in Africa. They live in the hotel for ten years.

6. Nick's mom and Nick spend all of the money and they don't tell Nick's dad. They buy lots of cars and houses. Nick's dad comes home. He is mad when he finds out that they spent all of the money.

7. Nick's mom asks him why he has so much money. He says that he has a rich friend who gave him a million dollars. She says Nick can keep the money if he gives her $1,000.

8. Nick buys a car and when he drives home he has a wreck. He doesn't have a license to drive because he is only twelve. His mom says he can't have a car for six years.

9. Nick sees someone who says they lost a lottery ticket. Nick gives the ticket to him. Nick watches TV that night. He sees that the ticket won a million dollars. He calls the man. The man gives Nick half of the money.

10. The lottery office doesn't give Nick the million dollars because he is too young. Nick's parents go with him and they get the money. Nick only gets $1,000.

THE DIRTY BABY

VOCABULARY PRACTICE

1	2	3
4	5	6
7	8	9 / 10
11	12	13
14	15	16

CHAPTER SIX
THE DIRTY BABY
VOCABULARY

1 CUTS

2 DIRTY BABY

3 FACE

4 BOWL

5 REFRIGERATOR

6 PIECES

7 FORK

8 PLATE

9 KNIFE

10 SPOON

11 ON TOP OF

12 EATS

13 COMES IN

14. WASHES

15. CLEAN BABY

16. THINGS

THE DIRTY BABY

THE DIRTY BABY

There is a baby. One day, he walks to the refrigerator and takes out some ice cream. He also takes out some chocolate milk. He walks to the table. There is a banana on the table. There is also a bowl and a knife.

He cuts the bananas in pieces and puts them in the bowl. He puts ice cream on top of the banana. He pours the chocolate milk on top of the ice cream.

He doesn't have a spoon or a fork. He eats with a knife. When he eats, the ice cream and the banana get on his face, arms and chest. The ice cream gets on his shirt, pants and shoes. There is ice cream and fruit everywhere. The baby is very dirty.

The baby's mother comes in the dining room. She sees the baby and screams, "What a dirty baby!" She grabs the baby and takes him to the bathroom. She takes off his clothes. She washes his head, cheeks, chest, arms, and legs. Finally, the baby is clean. The mother is happy because the baby is clean.

EXERCISE 1

WRITE TRUE OR FALSE TO THE LEFT OF THE NUMBER.

_____ 1. The baby can walk alone.

_____ 2. The baby walks to the refrigerator.

_____ 3. The banana is in the refrigerator.

_____ 4. The baby puts the banana on top of the ice cream.

_____ 5. The baby pours the chocolate milk on the floor.

_____ 6. The spoon and the fork are on the table.

_____ 7. The baby eats with a knife.

_____ 8. The baby's mother enters the dining room.

_____ 9. She yells, "What a dirty baby!"

_____ 10. The mother cleans the baby.

EXERCISE 2

FILL IN THE BLANKS WITH A WORD THAT MAKES THE SENTENCE TRUE.

1. The baby walks to the _____.

2. The baby takes out some _____.

3. On the table is a _____.

4. The baby cuts the _____ into pieces.

5. He pours _____ milk on top of everything.

6. There is not a spoon or a _____ on the table.

7. He gets ice cream on his_____.

8. The mother _____ when she enters the room.

9. The mother _____ the baby's head.

10. The mother is happy that the baby is finally _____.

44

EXERCISE 3

ANSWER THE QUESTIONS WITH SHORT ANSWERS.
(IF THE ANSWER ISN'T IN THE STORY, MAKE IT UP.)

1. What is the name of the baby?

2. Who takes out the chocolate milk?

3. Where does the baby find the ice cream?

4. What does the baby see on top of the table?

5. Why does the baby get dirty?

6. Why does the baby eat with a knife?

7. Who enters the room?

8. What does the mother do when she sees the baby?

9. Why does she wash the baby?

10. Why does the mother take off the baby's clothes?

EXERCISE 4

PUT THESE SENTENCES IN THE CORRECT ORDER.

_____ A knife, a bowl, and a banana are on the table.

_____ The baby cuts the banana.

_____ He walks to the refrigerator.

_____ He takes some ice cream out of the refrigerator.

_____ The mother washes the baby.

_____ The baby eats with a knife.

_____ He pours chocolate milk on top of the ice cream.

_____ What a dirty baby!

EXERCISE 5

REWRITE THE STORY IN YOUR OWN WORDS.

_____

_____

_____

_____

_____

_____

EXERCISE 6

RETELL THIS VERSION.

VERSION A

46

1

2

3

4

5

6

7

8

EXERCISE 8

WRITE YOUR OWN STORY.

_____

_____

_____

_____

_____

EXERCISE 9

RETELL THE FOLLOWING STORIES.

1. A dog is eating ice cream. Ice cream is everywhere. The dog runs away. The mother thinks the baby ate the ice cream.

2. The baby eats with a spoon and doesn't get dirty. The mother comes in and sees the baby eating. The mother gets mad at the baby because there is a little ice cream on the baby's face.

3. The mother and the baby are in a store. The baby throws ice cream on the floor. The baby pours chocolate milk on the floor. The baby pours chocolate milk on the mother . The mother and baby go home.

4. There are two babies. They are eating ice cream. Their father enters the room and sees the babies. The father yells, "Why are the babies eating ice cream alone?" The mother says, "They always eat alone."

5. The baby is in the park. He is eating ice cream. A cat goes to the baby and eats the baby's ice cream. The baby cries. The mother buys the baby more ice cream.

6. When the mother sees the baby, the baby runs away from home. The mother tries to catch the baby, but the baby runs too fast. The mother calls the police and they bring him home.

7. The baby is eating ice cream on a beach, and some people laugh at the baby. One man takes the baby and washes him in the ocean.

8. The baby is in the front of the house. He grabs some paint. He paints the house, his sister, and the window. The mother spanks the baby when she sees the dirty baby.

9. The mother and a baby are at a restaurant. The baby throws food on the floor while the mother is in the bathroom. The mother comes back and is very mad at the baby.

10. The baby is in Mexico. He is sitting on the floor. He is eating the bread that is on the floor. The mother sees the baby. She yells, "Don't eat the bread that is on the floor!"

THE THREE ELEPHANTS

VOCABULARY

1	2	3
4	5	6
7	8	9
10	11	12
13	14	

THE THREE ELEPHANTS

VOCABULARY

1 BREAKS	2 LIES DOWN	3 TASTES
4 BEAR	5 BROKEN	6 JUNGLE
7. MAD	8 WAITS	9 BEDROOM
10 ELEPHANT	11 KITCHEN	12 PEANUT
13 SOUP	14 GETS UP	

THE THREE ELEPHANTS

THE THREE ELEPHANTS

Three elephants live in a house in the middle of the jungle.

The mother elephant is in the kitchen. She is making peanut soup.

The father elephant and the baby elephant are in the dining room. They are waiting for the soup. The mother elephant comes to the dining room and gives them soup. They taste the soup. It is too hot. They go for a walk.

A girl named Jana is walking in the middle of the jungle. She sees the house and goes in. She goes to the dining room and tastes the soup. She doesn't like the soup, but she likes the peanuts. She eats all of the peanuts but she doesn't eat the soup.

She goes to the living room. She sits on a chair. The chair breaks.

She goes to the bedroom. She lies down on the bed. She goes to sleep.

The three elephants return home. They go in the dining room. They taste their soup. The soup doesn't have any peanuts. They are mad.

The elephants go to the living room. They see the broken chair. They are mad.

The elephants go to the bedroom. They see Jana. They scream. Jana gets up and runs away.

EXERCISE 1

WRITE TRUE OR FALSE TO THE LEFT OF THE NUMBER.

_____ 1. The three elephants live in the middle of the forest.

_____ 2. The three elephants live in a house.

_____ 3. The mother elephant prepares the soup in the kitchen.

_____ 4. The three elephants go for a walk.

_____ 5. Jana enters the three elephants' house.

_____ 6. Jana eats the soup and the peanuts.

_____ 7. Jana breaks the chair when she sits on it.

_____ 8. Jana goes to the bathroom.

_____ 9. Jana goes to sleep in the bedroom.

_____ 10. The three elephants eat the peanuts in the soup.

EXERCISE 2

FILL IN THE BLANKS WITH A WORD THAT MAKES THE SENTENCE TRUE.

1. The _____ elephants live in the middle of the jungle.
2. The mother elephant prepares soup in the _____.
3. The other elephants wait in the _____ room.
4. The elephants taste the peanut _____.
5. They go for a walk because the soup is too _____.
6. Jana is walking in the middle of the _____.
7. Jana _____ the house.
8. Jana eats all of the _____.
9. Jana goes to sleep on the _____.
10. The three elephants see the chair and they are _____.

52

EXERCISE 3

ANSWER THE QUESTIONS WITH SHORT ANSWERS.
(IF THE ANSWER ISN'T IN THE STORY, MAKE IT UP.)

1. Where do the elephants live?

2. Why do they live in a house?

3. Why does the mother make peanut soup?

4. Why don't they eat the soup?

5. What are the elephants wearing?

6. Why is Jana walking alone?

7. Why does she enter the house?

8. Why doesn't she eat the soup?

9. Why does the chair break?

10. Why are the three elephants mad?

EXERCISE 4

PUT THESE SENTENCES IN THE CORRECT ORDER.

_____ The elephants go for a walk.

_____ Jana breaks the chair and goes to sleep.

_____ The three elephants see the soup and are mad.

_____ There is a house in the middle of the jungle.

_____ The elephants see the chair. The girl runs away.

_____ The mother elephant prepares the soup in the kitchen.

_____ Jana tastes the soup.

_____ The elephants taste the soup.

EXERCISE 5

REWRITE THE STORY IN YOUR OWN WORDS.

_____

_____

_____

_____

_____

_____

EXERCISE 6

RETELL THIS VERSION.

VERSION A

EXERCISE 8

WRITE YOUR OWN STORY.

_____

_____

_____

_____

_____

_____

EXERCISE 9

RETELL THE FOLLOWING STORIES.

1. The elephants are bears who live in the middle of the forest.

2. The three elephants visit the girl's house. They eat a lot of food. They lie down on her bed and break it.

3. An elephant lives in Russia. He lives in a house. He has a lot of money. A girl goes in his house. She eats his food. She sits in his chair. She goes to sleep in his chair. He returns. He is mad.

4. An elephant and a bear live in a house in the middle of the beach. They go for a walk. They see a girl. They see another bear. They return home. The door is open. They go in the house and no one is there.

5. A girl goes to Italy. She goes into a house. She sees pictures of elephants that live there. She grabs the pictures and goes home.

6. The girl goes to the elephants' house when they are home. They invite her to eat. They show her the house. They go to her house. Her mother says they can't eat with them.

7. A girl lives in a house with three bears. She has her own bedroom. The girl helps the bears. She prepares their soup. She cleans the house. The bears are happy because the girl lives with them.

8. A girl and a bear take a plane to France. They go to Paris. The girl goes to a restaurant with the bear. A man says the bear can't eat in the restaurant. They go home.

9. There are three houses. Elephants live in one of the houses. Bears live in another house. A girl lives in the other house. The bears, elephants and the girl go for a walk to the beach. They swim. They go back home.

10. There are three houses, one for each elephant. Jana goes in each house. The first house is clean. The second and third houses are dirty. She cleans the dirty houses. The elephants return. They are happy because their houses are clean.

CHAPTER EIGHT

THE MOON STORY

VOCABULARY

1	2	3
4	5	6
7	8	9
10	11	12
13	14	15
16	17	

THE MOON STORY

VOCABULARY

1	BREAD	2	GETS IN	3	SPACE SHIP
4	FOREIGN LANGUAGE	5	MENU	6	MUSTARD
7	POCKET	8	ROCKET	9	FLIES
10	HAMBURGER	11	FOOD	12	PEOPLE
13	TAKES OFF	14	LANDS	15	MOON
16	RESTAURANT	17	WAITRESS		

THE MOON STORY

THE MOON STORY

Fred lives in Florida. He wants to go to the moon. He goes to Cape Canaveral and gets in a rocket. He flies to the moon. He lands on the moon. He gets out of the rocket and looks around. He goes for a walk. After a while, he sees a restaurant. He enters the restaurant. There are a lot of moon people in the restaurant. He goes to a table and sits down.

A waitress goes to the table. She has a menu in her hand. She gives him the menu. He opens it and reads it. He doesn't understand any of the menu. He closes the menu and says that he doesn't understand it because it is written in another language. The waitress says, "What do you want?"

Fred says, "I want a hamburger."

"What is a hamburger?" responds the waitress.

"It has two pieces of bread, meat, tomatoes, lettuce, catsup, and mustard. It is American food."

The waitress answers, "This isn't America. We don't have American food here."

Fred says, "What do you have?"

She replies, "We only have moon food here."

"I want some."

The waitress leaves and comes back with a plate of moon food. Fred looks at the food and can't believe it. Part of the food looks horrible, but the other part looks good. He eats the good part but doesn't eat the bad part.

He puts his hand in his pocket. He remembers that he is on the moon and he doesn't have any moon money. He gets up and runs outside to his rocket. He gets in and goes back to planet Earth.

EXERCISE 1

WRITE TRUE OR FALSE TO THE LEFT OF THE NUMBER.

_____ 1. Fred lives in Florida.

_____ 2. Fred goes to the moon in a rocket.

_____ 3. He goes to a restaurant in Florida.

_____ 4. The waitress lives on the moon.

_____ 5. Fred understands the menu.

_____ 6. Fred orders a hamburger.

_____ 7. Fred eats the hamburger.

_____ 8. Fred eats all of the moon food.

_____ 9. He doesn't have any moon money.

_____ 10. He goes back to Earth.

EXERCISE 2

PUT THESE SENTENCES IN THE CORRECT ORDER.

_____ Fred receives moon food.

_____ He walks to the restaurant.

_____ He goes to the moon in a rocket.

_____ He lands on the moon.

_____ He returns to Earth.

_____ He orders a hamburger.

_____ He has no moon money.

_____ He looks at the moon menu.

EXERCISE 3

FILL IN THE BLANKS WITH A WORD THAT MAKES THE SENTENCE TRUE.

1. Fred wants to go to the _____.
2. Fred flies to the moon in a_____.
3. He lands on the moon and goes for a _____.
4. After a while, he enters the_____.
5. Fred looks at the menu but he doesn't _____ it.
6. He finally orders a_____.
7. The waitress brings him _____ food.
8. Part of the food looks bad but the other part looks _____.
9. He only eats the _____ part.
10. Fred gets in his _____ and goes back to Earth.

EXERCISE 4

ANSWER THE QUESTIONS WITH SHORT ANSWERS.
(IF THE ANSWER ISN'T IN THE STORY, MAKE IT UP.)

1. Why does Fred want to go to the moon?
2. What is Fred looking for on the moon?
3. Why does he go in the restaurant?
4. Why can't he read the menu?
5. Why doesn't the waitress know what a hamburger is?
6. What kind of food does she bring him?
7. Why does she bring him moon food?
8. Why doesn't he eat all of the moon food?
9. Why doesn't he pay for the food?
10. Why does he go back to Earth?

EXERCISE 5

REWRITE THE STORY IN YOUR OWN WORDS.

_____

_____

_____

_____

EXERCISE 8

WRITE YOUR OWN STORY.

_____

_____

_____

_____

_____

_____

_____

EXERCISE 9

RETELL THE FOLLOWING STORIES.

1. Fred goes to Mexico. He orders a taco. He doesn't eat it. He has no money and leaves.

2. A person from the moon goes to the United States. He goes in a restaurant. He orders moon food. The waitress doesn't understand. She brings him a hamburger. He eats it and l e a v e s because he has no money.

3. Fred goes to Australia in a rocket. He thinks he is on the moon. He is surprised when the people speak English.

4. Fred and his cat go to the moon. They walk a lot on the moon. They don't see anything. They go to Mars. There are lots of cats on Mars. They pick up a cat and take it back to Earth.

5. Fred takes a boat to Hawaii. He goes around the island. He sees a beautiful beach. He buys a small house. He lives in the house for many years.

6. A moon man goes to Fred's house. Fred gives him a hamburger. The moon man likes the hamburger. Fred takes him to a baseball game. The moon man doesn't like baseball. He gets in his rocket and goes back to the moon.

7. When he lands on the moon he sees lots of trees, rivers, mountains, and oceans. He swims in the rivers and the oceans. He climbs a mountain. He looks for people. He doesn't find anyone on the moon. He goes back to Earth.

8. Fred marries the waitress and stays on the moon. He buys a moon house. They have moon children. He never goes back to Earth.

9. Fred goes to South America. He tastes the food there. He doesn't like it. It is horrible. He goes to Africa. He tries the food there. He likes it. He buys a lot of food. He takes it home with him.

10. He finds a moon dog and takes him back to Earth. The moon dog can fly. The dog flies around the world. People are surprised to see a dog that can fly.

THE DATE

VOCABULARY

THE DATE

VOCABULARY

1 ARRIVES

2 DANCE

3 DRYING

4 PICK UP

5 SHOWER

6 START

7 WEAR

8 ASK

9 DRESSING

10 KNOCKS ON DOOR

11 READY

12 SOFT DRINK

13 TRIPS

14 CALLS

15 DRIVES

16 MAKEUP

17 SHAVES

18 SPILLS

THE DATE

THE DATE

Von calls Shelly and asks her if she wants to go to the dance. Shelly says that she wants to go. He is going to pick her up at 9:00. The dance starts at 9:30.

At 8:00, Von gets ready for the dance. He showers, shaves, and washes his hair. He puts on deodorant and brushes his teeth. He puts on underwear, pants, a shirt, socks and shoes.

He leaves the house and gets in the car. He drives to Shelly's house.

When he arrives, he knocks on the door. Her mom opens the door and he goes in.

Shelly is still in the bathroom. She is drying and curling her hair. She is also dressing and putting on her makeup. She is wearing a new dress.

Shelly is ready. They leave the house and go to the car. They go to the dance. They dance for two hours without stopping.

Von gets Shelly a soft drink. When he comes back, he trips and falls. The drink goes all over Shelly's new dress. She screams, "Take me home!"

He drives her home. When they arrive, Shelly opens the door of the car and yells, "I never want to go to a dance with you again!"

EXERCISE 1

WRITE TRUE OR FALSE TO THE LEFT OF THE NUMBER.

_____ 1. Shelly wants to go to the dance.

_____ 2. The dance starts at 9:00.

_____ 3. Von drives to Shelly's house at 8:00.

_____ 4. Von showers and shaves.

_____ 5. When Von arrives, Shelly is still in the bathroom.

_____ 6. Shelly gets dressed in the kitchen.

_____ 7. Shelly is wearing a new dress.

_____ 8. Shelly gets a soft drink for Von.

_____ 9. Von spills the drink on Shelly.

_____ 10. Shelly wants to go to a dance with Von next week.

EXERCISE 2

FILL IN THE BLANKS WITH A WORD THAT MAKES THE SENTENCE TRUE..

1. Von invites Shelly to go to the _____.

2. The dance _____ at 9:30.

3. Von puts on deodorant and _____ his teeth.

4. Shelly's mother _____ the door.

5. Shelly is still in the _____.

6. Shelly puts on her _____ in the bathroom.

7. Shelly is going to wear a new _____.

8. They dance for two _____.

9. When Von brings a drink, he trips and _____ it.

10. Shelly doesn't want to go to a _____ with Von any more.

68

EXERCISE 3
ANSWER THE QUESTIONS WITH SHORT ANSWERS.
(IF THE ANSWER ISN'T IN THE STORY, MAKE IT UP.)

1. Why does Von call Shelly?

2. Why does Von go to the dance?

3. Why does Von brush his teeth?

4. Where does he go to pick up Shelly?

5. Why isn't Shelly ready?

6. Why does Shelly's mom open the door?

7. Why does Von drive to the dance?

8. Why do they dance for two hours?

9. What does Von trip over?

10. Why doesn't Shelly want to go to another dance with Von?

EXERCISE 4
PUT THESE SENTENCES IN THE CORRECT ORDER.

_____Shelly is in the bathroom.

_____Von calls Shelly.

_____They dance for two hours.

_____Von drives to Shelly's house.

_____Shelly is ready to go to the dance.

_____Von takes Shelly home.

_____Von is in the bathroom.

_____Von spills the soft drink on Shelly.

EXERCISE 5
REWRITE THE STORY IN YOUR OWN WORDS.

_____

_____

_____

_____

_____

_____

69

1

2

3

4

5

6

EXERCISE 8
REWRITE YOUR OWN STORY.

_____

_____

_____

_____

_____

_____

EXERCISE 9
RETELL THE FOLLOWING STORIES.

1. Shelly asks Von to go to the dance. They don't go to the dance. They go to a movie. Shelly doesn't like the movie. She is mad and wants to go home. Von takes her home.

2. Shelly spills the soft drink on Von. He says that it is all right. He goes to the bathroom and cleans his clothes. He goes back to the dance and dances with Shelly. Later they go home.

3. Von asks Shelly to go to Germany. They take a plane to Germany. They speak German. They get married in Germany. They buy a house in Germany and stay there.

4. Von and Shelly are in Mexico. Von speaks Spanish, but Shelly doesn't. Von talks to a girl. Shelly thinks he is talking about her. She gets mad and takes a plane back to the United States.

5. Von and Shelly go out to eat before the dance. All goes well at the dance. When they are going home, the car runs out of gas. It is late. There is no place to buy gas. They walk home.

6. Von sees another girl at the dance. He dances with her all night. Shelly is very mad. She takes Von's car and drives downtown. She finds another boy. She drives Von's car to her house.

7. Von goes to the dance in a t-shirt and shorts. Shelly goes in a beautiful dress. Shelly doesn't dance with Von. She dances with a boy who is wearing a suit. She goes home with the boy in a suit.

8. Von is going to go out with two girls on the same night. He goes out with Sandra at 7:00. He wants to go out with Shelly at 9:00. They go to Sandra's house after the movie. Shelly calls Von while he is at Sandra's house. She tells him that her mom says she can't go out with him that night.

9. It is 10:00 at night. Von sees a girl walking along the street. He asks her if she wants to ride in his car. She says that she wants to and she gets in the car. He drives very fast. The girl is afraid and gets out and walks.

10. Von invites Shelly to his house to study French. Von says that he knows French very well. He says he lived in France for two years. He doesn't know anything about French. He tells her the wrong answers. She doesn't go to his house again.

CHAPTER TEN

WALLY AND AMY

VOCABULARY

WALLY AND AMY

VOCABULARY

1 CAR

2 SKINNY

3 STOP

4 FRIENDS

5 NEW

6 SLOW

7 TALL

8 SHORT

9 YESTERDAY, TODAY

10 FAST

WALLY AND AMY

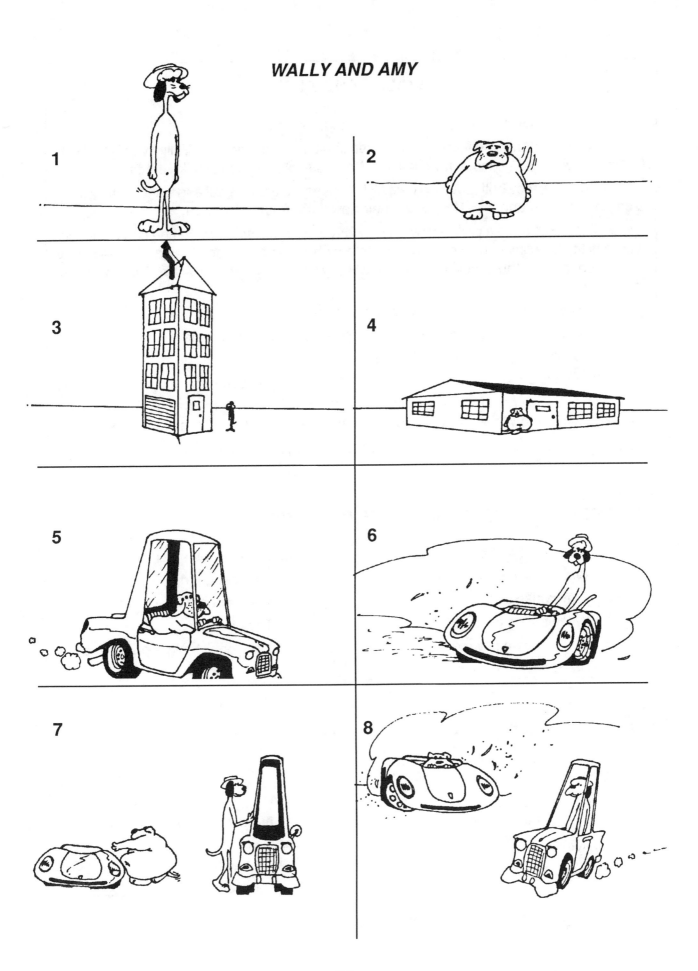

WALLY AND AMY

Amy is a tall, skinny dog. Wally is a short, fat dog.

Wally and Amy are friends. Amy lives in a tall, skinny house. Wally lives in a short, fat house. Amy is tall and can walk fast. Wally is short and can't walk very fast.

One day, they both buy new cars. Wally buys a car that is tall and skinny. Amy buys a car that is short and fat. They drive their new cars around the town.

They both have a problem when they drive. Wally is so short that he can't see very well in his tall, skinny car. Amy is too tall for her short, fat car. When they are driving, they pass each other on the street. Amy honks at Wally and Wally honks at Amy. They both stop their cars and run to each other.

Amy yells, "When did you get that new car?"

Wally replies, "I just bought it today. When did you get your new car?"

She tells him, "I just bought it today."

"I don't like my car. Let's trade cars," they both say together.

They trade cars and now neither one of them has a problem driving. Amy drives a tall, skinny car and Wally drives a short, fat car. They can now drive much better.

EXERCISE 1
WRITE TRUE OR FALSE TO THE LEFT OF THE NUMBER.

_____ 1. Amy is tall and skinny.

_____ 2. Wally is short and fat.

_____ 3. Amy walks fast.

_____ 4. Wally drives fast.

_____ 5. Wally buys a new car.

_____ 6. Wally drives a tall car.

_____ 7. Amy bought her car today.

_____ 8. Wally bought his car yesterday.

_____ 9. They trade cars.

_____ 10. They don't have a problem driving now.

EXERCISE 2
FILL IN THE BLANKS WITH A WORD THAT MAKES THE SENTENCE TRUE.

1. Amy is a tall_____.

2. Wally is_____.

3. Wally lives in a short, fat_____.

4. Amy lives in a tall, skinny _____.

5. They have a problem when they _____.

6. Amy is too _____ for her short, fat car.

7. They _____ each other on the street.

8. Amy asks Wally where he got his new _____.

9. They decide to _____ cars.

10. Wally now drives a short, _____ car.

EXERCISE 3
ANSWER THE QUESTIONS WITH SHORT ANSWERS.
(IF IT ISN'T IN THE STORY, MAKE IT UP)

1. Who is short and fat?

2. Why can Amy walk fast?

3. Why does Wally walk slowly?

4. Why does Amy buy a short, fat car?

5. Why does Wally have a problem when he drives?

6. Why does Amy have a car?

7. When did Wally buy his new car?

8. Why did they trade cars?

9. Why did they honk at each other?

10. Why was their trade a good one?

EXERCISE 4
PUT THESE SENTENCES IN THE CORRECT ORDER.

_____They trade cars.

_____Wally is a short, fat dog.

_____Wally lives in a short, fat house.

_____Amy is a tall, skinny dog.

_____Amy lives in a tall, skinny house.

_____They drive the new cars after they traded.

_____Wally buys a long, skinny car.

_____Amy buys a short, fat car.

EXERCISE 5
REWRITE THE STORY IN YOUR OWN WORDS.

_____

_____

_____

_____

_____

_____

1

2

3

4

5

6

1

2

3

4

5

6

EXERCISE 8

WRITE YOUR OWN STORY.

_____

_____

_____

_____

_____

EXERCISE 9

RETELL THE FOLLOWING STORIES.

1. Two boys go the mountains. They have a lot of food. Wally has a taco. Ralph has pancakes. They look at their food. Ralph doesn't like pancakes. Wally doesn't like tacos. Ralph and Wally trade food.

2. There are two cats. One lives in a house in Brazil. He doesn't like the heat of Brazil. The other cat lives in a house in Canada. It is cold in Canada. He doesn't like the cold of Canada. They trade houses.

3. Amy and Wally live in the same house. Wally has a black room and Amy has a red room. Wally paints his room red and Amy paints her room black.

4. Amy is rich and Wally is poor. Amy buys a new car. Wally walks. Amy lives in a big house. Wally sleeps on the street. Amy and Wally get married. Wally is happy because he doesn't sleep in the street anymore.

5. Amy goes to school with a dirty shirt. Wally goes up to Amy and tells her that she has a dirty shirt. Wally has an extra shirt. He gives her the shirt. She wears the shirt the rest of the day.

6. Amy and Wally go to a restaurant to eat dinner. Amy orders a hamburger and Wally orders fish. They taste their food. They don't like the food that they have. They trade their food.

7. Wally likes to play the piano. Amy likes to play the flute. They play their musical instruments every day. Amy goes to Wally's house. He plays a song for her. He gives her the music to the song and she plays the same song on the flute.

8. Amy speaks Spanish and Wally speaks French. They both want to learn another language. Wally starts to speak French to Amy and Amy speaks Spanish to Wally. After a few months, they both speak French one week and speak Spanish the next week.

9. Wally and Amy always go to the mountains to ski. They ski every weekend during the winter. One day they decide to try ice skating. The next winter they don't ski any more. They go ice skating every weekend.

10. Amy goes to Mexico and lives with a family for a year. Wally goes to France and lives with a family for a year. They return to the United States and tell each other about their experiences.

THE BOY WHO IS LATE

VOCABULARY

1	2	3
4	5	6
7	8	9
10	11	12
13	14	

CHAPTER ELEVEN
THE BOY WHO IS LATE
VOCABULARY

1	ALIVE	2	BLOCK	3.	GIRLFRIEND
4	MORNING	5	ROOM	6	SLEEPY
7	BORED	8	GUN	9	KILL
10	BANK	11	TIME	12	LUCKY
13	ROB	14	SITTING		

THE BOY WHO IS LATE

THE BOY WHO IS LATE

It is 12 o'clock at night. Jim is sitting on his bed. He is bored. He is not sleepy. He sees an open window. He walks to the window and jumps out the window. He runs to his girlfriend's house. She only lives two blocks away.

He knocks on the door. His girlfriend answers the door. She invites him to come in. They watch TV for two hours. Jim looks at his watch. It is two o'clock in the morning. He says, "It is very late. I need to go home." He stands up and runs to his house. The window is still open. He goes to his window and enters the room.

When he is in the room, he looks on his bed. His parents are sitting on the bed. His dad is looking at his watch. He says, "It is two o'clock in the morning. Why are you coming home now?"

Jim says, "I looked out the window. A man was robbing a bank. I ran out and tried to catch the robber. I ran after him for three hours. He stopped. When I saw that he had a gun, I came home as fast as possible. I am lucky to be alive."

The mother says, "You are very lucky. I am glad that he didn't kill you."

EXERCISE 1
WRITE TRUE OR FALSE TO THE LEFT OF THE NUMBER.

_____ 1. Jim is in his room.

_____ 2. Jim leaves through the door.

_____ 3. He drives downtown.

_____ 4. He goes to his girlfriend's house.

_____ 5. They watch TV for three hours.

_____ 6. Jim goes home at 2 a.m.

_____ 7. When he goes in his room, his parents are on his bed.

_____ 8. He told his parents that he ran after a robber.

_____ 9. His mother told him to not run after bank robbers.

_____ 10. Jim ran after the robber for one hour.

EXERCISE 2
FILL IN THE BLANKS WITH A WORD THAT MAKES THE SENTENCE TRUE.

1. _____ is sitting on his bed.
2. Jim runs to his _____ house.
3. He leaves through an _____ window.
4. They watch _____ for two hours.
5. When he arrives home, the window is still _____.
6. Jim's _____ are sitting on the bed.
7. His dad is looking at his _____.
8. Jim said that he ran after the robber for _____ hours.
9. Jim said the robber had a _____.
10. His mother said that Jim is _____ to be alive.

84

EXERCISE 3
ANSWER THE QUESTIONS WITH SHORT ANSWERS
(IF IT ISN'T IN THE STORY, MAKE IT UP)

1. Why doesn't Jim go to sleep?

2. Why doesn't he go out the door?

3. Where does Jim go when he leaves the house?

4. What do Jim and his girlfriend do?

5. Why does Jim need to go home?

6. Why doesn't his girlfriend need to go home?

7. Why are his parents in his room?

8. Why is Jim late?

9. Why does his mother say that he is lucky to be alive?

10. Why is Jim lucky?

EXERCISE 4

PUT THESE SENTENCES IN THE CORRECT ORDER.

_____ Jim runs after the robber.
_____ They watch TV for two hours.
_____ It is 12:00 p.m., and Jim is sitting in bed.
_____ He leaves through the window.

_____ He enters the room through the window.
_____ His mother says that Jim is lucky to be alive.
_____ His parents are sitting on his bed.
_____ Jim runs to his girlfriend's house.

EXERCISE 5

REWRITE THE STORY IN YOUR OWN WORDS.

_____

_____

_____

_____

_____

_____

EXERCISE 6

RETELL THIS VERSION.

VERSION A

EXERCISE 8

WRITE YOUR OWN STORY.

_____

_____

_____

_____

_____

_____

EXERCISE 9

RETELL THE FOLLOWING STORIES.

1. It is in the afternoon and Jim goes to the park. He sees a robber and runs home. His mother asks him why he was running.

2. Jim goes to the house of a friend. They go out to a restaurant and eat pizza. They get back home at three in the morning. Jim goes home and his parents are not home.

3. I went to the store at midnight. I bought some food and soft drinks. I went to my girl friend's house to watch TV. When I was watching TV, my parents called. I went home.

4. You leave the house and go to the mountains. You go to a lake and go water skiing. You eat lunch in the mountains. You return home. Your parents are waiting for you.

5. Jim and Gus go to the park. They see a girl. They go to her house and listen to the radio. They dance for one hour. It is eleven o'clock at night. Jim goes back to his house and Gus goes back to his house.

6. Jim sees a robber, and invites the robber to go with him to watch TV at his girlfriend's house. The robber goes with him and they all watch TV for two hours.

7. Jim sees his parents leaving the house through the window. He asks them where they are going. They say they are going to a movie. Jim says it is very late. The parents stay home.

8. When Jim is running after the robber, the police see him and think he is the robber. They talk to him. Later, they take him home and tell his parents why Jim was late.

9. Jim's parents listen to his story about the robber. They don't believe him. They tell him they know that he was at his girlfriend's house and that he can't see her for a week.

10. Jim tells his parents that a bird came into his room and took one of his records. He ran after the bird for two hours. The bird finally dropped the record and he got it back. His parents were glad he was being honest.

CHAPTER TWELVE
CURTIS AND LORI
VOCABULARY

1	2	3	4	5	6	7

8	9	10
11	12	13
14	15	16
17	18	

CURTIS AND LORI

VOCABULARY

1 Sunday   2 Monday   3 Tuesday   4 Wednesday   5 Thursday   6 Friday   7 Saturday

8 LOVE	9 OFFICE	10 TENNIS
11 CARDS	12 GOLF	13 MARRIED
14 PLAY	15 WORK	16 CHURCH
17 SWIM	18 UPSET	

CURTIS AND LORI

CURTIS AND LORI

Curtis and Lori are married. Curtis is too busy. Lori is too busy. Here is Curtis' and Lori's schedule:

Sunday	Curtis and Lori go to church.
Monday	Lori flies to New York for business.
Tuesday	Lori flies back home.
Wednesday	Curtis works at the office until late.
Thursday	Curtis plays cards with his friends.
Friday	Lori goes swimming after work.
Saturday	Curtis plays golf.

Lori and Curtis are upset that they don't have more time to spend with each other. Lori says, "Come home more and spend time with me."

Curtis responds, "We have lots of money. What more do we want?"

"I want time with you."

"We will spend more time with each other. On Fridays, we will eat in a nice restaurant together. On Sundays, we can go to church together. On Thursdays, we can watch TV together, and on Saturdays, we will play tennis together. What do you think of that?"

Lori runs to Curtis and hugs him, kisses him, and says, " I love you."

EXERCISE 1
WRITE TRUE OR FALSE TO THE LEFT OF THE NUMBER.

_____ 1. Curtis and Lori are married.

_____ 2. Curtis is bored.

_____ 3. Lori flies to New York on Tuesday.

_____ 4. Curtis plays golf on Saturday.

_____ 5. Curtis goes to New York for business.

_____ 6. Curtis gives his wife lots of money.

_____ 7. Lori wants more money.

_____ 8. Lori and Curtis want more time with each other.

_____ 9. Curtis runs to Lori and hugs her.

_____ 10. Lori says, "I love you."

EXERCISE 2
FILL IN THE BLANKS WITH A WORD THAT MAKES THE SENTENCE TRUE.

1. Lori and Curtis are_____.
2. Lori goes to New York on_____.
3. On Wednesday, Curtis works late at the _____.
4. On Saturday, he_____golf.
5. On Thursday, he plays_____ with friends.
6. Lori wants more of his_____.

7. On Fridays, they are going to _____ together.
8. On_____, they are going to play tennis.
9. On Thursdays, they are going to_____TV.
10. Lori runs to Curtis and _____ him.

92

EXERCISE 3
ANSWER THE QUESTIONS WITH SHORT ANSWERS.
(IF THE ANSWER ISN'T IN THE STORY, MAKE IT UP.)

1. Why are Curtis and Lori busy?

2. Why does she go to New York?

3. Why does he work late on Wednesdays?

4. Why do they spend so little time with each other?

5. Where does Lori fly for business?

6. Why are Curtis and Lori going to spend more time with each other?

7. What are they going to do on Thursday?

8. When are they going to eat in a nice restaurant?

9. Why does Lori hug and kiss Curtis?

EXERCISE 4
PUT THESE SENTENCES IN THE CORRECT ORDER.

____Curtis works late.

____Curtis goes to church.

____Lori and Curtis are married.

____Lori and Curtis kiss and she says, "I love you."

____Lori swims.

____Curtis plays golf.

____Lori returns from New York.

____They are going to eat in a nice restaurant.

____Lori goes to New York.

____Curtis plays cards with his friends.

EXERCISE 5
REWRITE THE STORY IN YOUR OWN WORDS.

_____

_____

_____

_____

_____

_____

EXERCISE 6

RETELL THIS VERSION.

VERSION A

EXERCISE 8

WRITE YOUR OWN STORY.

_____

_____

_____

_____

_____

_____

EXERCISE 9

RETELL THE FOLLOWING STORIES.

1. Curtis stays at home and Lori is busy. She works and plays golf. She swims and plays tennis. Curtis never leaves the house. He just sleeps, eats and watches TV.

2. On weekends, Curtis plays golf. On Mondays, he flies to Chicago. On Tuesdays, he plays tennis. On Wednesdays, he swims. On Thursdays, he watches TV. On Fridays, he goes out with his wife.

3. Lori lives in Los Angeles and Curtis lives in Chicago. They both fly to New York on Tuesdays and play golf and tennis together.

4. Curtis doesn't want to change. Lori marries another man. She goes out every night of the week. He stays home.

5. Lori gives Curtis more money and he is happy. He goes out with his friends every day. He goes shopping every morning. He buys Lori lots of clothing.

6. Kim lives in France. She is learning French. Curtis lives in Spain. He is learning Spanish. They both live in Europe for one year. Afterwards, they move to New York. They teach each other their new languages.

7. Curtis works every day of the week. Kim works at night every day of the week. They are together only on weekends.

8. Lori and Curtis go to Canada. They get new jobs. Curtis is a salesman. Lori is a nurse.

9. Lori doesn't want to live with Curtis anymore. She goes home and lives with her parents.

10. Lori and Curtis play golf on Tuesdays and Thursdays. They swim on Mondays and Wednesdays. They watch TV on Fridays and Saturdays.

AUTHOR'S CHOICE !

Triple Expanded 2nd Edition!

INSTRUCTOR'S NOTEBOOK
How to Apply TPR For Best Results
TRIPLE EXPANDED SECOND EDITION

BEST-SELLER!

For 20 years, Ramiro Garcia has successfully applied the **Total Physical Response** in his high school and adult language classes.

Four NEW Chapters in the **Triple Expanded Second Edition** (288 pages):

- **Speaking, Reading, and Writing**
- **How to Create Your Own TPR Lessons.**
- More than **200 TPR scenarios** for **beginning** and **advanced students.**
- **TPR Games** for all age groups
- **TPR Testing** for **all skills** including **oral proficiency.**

In this illustrated book, Ramiro shares the tips and tricks that he has discovered in using TPR with hundreds of students. No matter what language you teach, including **ESL** and the **sign language of the deaf,** you will enjoy this insightful and humorous book.

  To order these books, Write, Call, or Fax:

Sky Oaks Productions, Inc.
P.O. Box 1102
Los Gatos, CA 95031-1102
PH: (408) 395-7600 • FAX: (408) 395-8440

Hot off the press!

THE GRAPHICS BOOK
For **All** Languages and Students of **All** Ages
by
RAMIRO GARCIA
edited by
JAMES J. ASHER

Here is the exciting sequel to my **Instructor's Notebook**.

Your students understand a huge chunk of the target language because you used TPR. Now, with my new *graphics* book, you can follow up with **300 drawings** on tear-out strips and sheets that help your students *zoom ahead* with **more vocabulary, grammar, talking, reading** and **writing** in the target language.

In this book, you will receive **step-by-step guidance** in how to apply the *graphics* effectively with **children and adults** acquiring **any language** including **ESL.**

As an **extra bonus**, I provide you with **60 multiple-choice graphic tests for beginning and intermediate students in your choice of English, Spanish, French or German.**

Examine this exciting *graphics* book for 30 days and if you are not completely satisfied, return it in salable condition for a full refund, with no questions asked.

Publisher's Note: Without a doubt, this is one of the most cost-effective TPR books we've *ever* published. Only <u>one</u> book is needed to teach <u>*an entire class*</u> — you don't need to buy anything else to use Ramiro's fantastic TPR Strips and Graphic Sheets!

—*James J. Asher*

AUTHOR'S CHOICE !

Make your own TPR Lessons!

The Command Book
Stephen M. Silvers

**Edited by
James J. Asher**

The Command Book is a dictionary of more than **2,000 vocabulary words most frequently used** in beginning and intermediate ESL/FL **textbooks.** What makes **The Command Book** unique is that each entry has several shades of lexical and grammatical meaning — and each meaning is presented in the powerful **Total Physical Response** format developed by James J. Asher. For Example:

> **Anywhere   Sit (stand) anywhere you wish.**

You have at your fingertips in **The Command Book** more than **10,000 Commands** for creating TPR lessons tailor-made for your students. Each entry is in **alphabetical order** for easy reference.

If you have tried TPR with your students, you know how effective the procedure is in helping students *internalize new vocabulary* and *grammar* quickly, effortlessly, and with amazing long-term retention. **The Command Book** is a **giant resource book** (more than **300 pages**) that you will use with pleasure every day.

HOT OFF THE PRESS!

LISTEN AND PERFORM
TPR Student Notebook
by
STEPHEN MARK SILVERS
Edited by
James J. Asher

You may now order this popular Student Notebook in your choice of **ENGLISH**, **SPANISH** or **FRENCH**!

Your students of **all ages** will enjoy more than 150 exciting pages of stimulating right brain **Total Physical Response** exercises such as:

- drawing   • pointing
- matching   • moving people,
- touching   places, and things.

With the **Student Notebook** and companion **Cassette**, each of your students can perform alone at their desks or at home to advance from comprehension to sophisticated skills of speaking, reading, and writing!

Ideal for multi-level classes and as a self-study book for students who have some skill in **English, Spanish, or French,** but don't have time to study in a formal language class.

 To order these books, Write, Call, or Fax:

Sky Oaks Productions, Inc.
P.O. Box 1102
Los Gatos, CA 95031-1102
PH: (408) 395-7600 • FAX: (408) 395-8440

AUTHOR'S CHOICE !

Look, I Can Talk!
by Blaine Ray

Student Notebook in English, Spanish, French or German

Here is an effective **TPR** story-telling technique that **zooms** your students into *talking, reading,* and *writing.* It works beautifully with beginning, intermediate and yes, — even advanced students.

Step-by-step, Blaine Ray shows you how to tell a story with **physical actions,** then have your students *tell the story to each other* in their own words **using the target language,** then **act** it out, **write** it and **read** it.

Each **Student Notebook** comes in your choice of *English, Spanish, French* or *German* and has

✔ 12 main stories

✔ 24 additional action-packed picture stories

✔ Many options for retelling each story

✔ Reading and writing exercises galore.

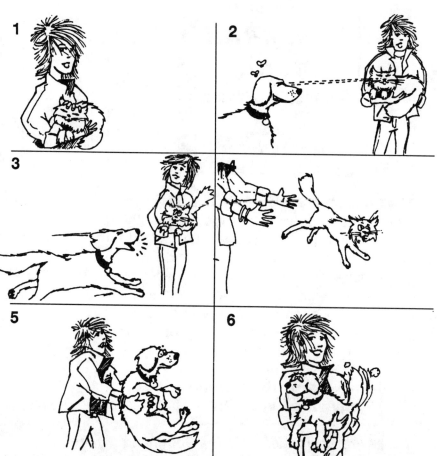

Blaine ***personally guarantees*** that each of your students will eagerly tell stories in the target language by using the **Student Notebook.**

To insure rapid student success, follow the thirteen magic steps explained in Blaine Ray's **Teacher's Guidebook** and then work with your students story-by-story with the easy-to-use **Overhead Transparencies.**